KT-366-961

INTRODUCTION

The ability to sight-read fluently is a most important part of your training as a violinist, whether you intend to play professionally, or simply for enjoyment. Yet the *study* of sight-reading is often badly neglected by young players and is frequently regarded as no more than a rather unpleasant side-line. If you become a *good* sight-reader you will be able to learn pieces more quickly, and play in ensembles and orchestras with confidence and assurance. Also, in grade examinations, good performance in the sight-reading test will result in useful extra marks!

Using the workbook

The purpose of this workbook is to incorporate sight-reading regularly into your practice and lessons, and to help you prepare for the sight-reading test in grade examinations. It offers you a progressive series of enjoyable and stimulating stages in which, with careful work, you should show considerable improvement from week to week.

Each stage consists of two parts: firstly, exercises which you should prepare in advance, along with a short piece with questions; and secondly, an unprepared test, to be found at the end of the book.

Your teacher will mark your work according to accuracy. Each stage carries a maximum of 50 marks and your work will be assessed as follows:

> 2 marks for each of the six questions relating to the prepared piece (total 12)
> 18 marks for the prepared piece itself.
> 20 marks for the unprepared test. (Teachers should devise a similar series of questions for the unprepared test, and take the answers into account when allocating a final mark.)

Space is given at the end of each stage for you to keep a running total of your marks as you progress. If you are scoring 40 or more each time you are doing well!

At the top of the first page in each stage you will see one or two new features to be introduced. There are then normally four different types of exercise:

1 **Rhythmic exercises** It is very important that you should be able to feel and maintain a steady beat. These exercises will help develop this ability. There are at least four ways of doing these exercises: clap or tap the lower line (the beat) while singing the upper line to 'la'; tap the lower line with your foot and clap the upper line; on a table or flat surface, tap the lower line with one hand and the upper line with the other; 'play' the lower line on a metronome and clap or tap the upper line.

2 **Melodic exercises** Fluent sight-reading depends on recognising melodic shapes at first glance. These shapes are often related to scales and arpeggios. Before you begin, always notice the *key-signature* and the notes affected by it, then work out the finger patterns on the finger board.

3 **A prepared piece with questions** You should prepare carefully both the piece and the questions, which are to help you think about and understand the piece before you play it. Put your answers in the spaces provided.

4 **An unprepared piece** Finally, your teacher will give you an *unprepared* test to be read at *sight*. Make sure you have read the *Sight-reading Checklist* on page 17 before you begin each piece.

Remember to count throughout each piece and to keep going at a steady and even tempo. Always try to look ahead, at least to the next note or beat.

NAME

EXAMINATION RECORD

Grade	Date	Mark

TEACHER'S NAME

TELEPHONE

© 1993 by Faber Music Ltd
First published in 1993 by Faber Music Ltd
3 Queen Square London WC1N 3AU
Design and typography by James Butler
Cover illustration by Drew Hillier
Music and text set by Silverfen
Printed in England by Caligraving Ltd
All rights reserved

ISBN 0-571-51386-7

STAGE 1

C major

RHYTHMIC EXERCISES

MELODIC EXERCISES

©1993 by Faber Music Ltd

This music is copyright. Photocopying is illegal.

PREPARED PIECE

		Marks*
1	What does $\frac{4}{4}$ indicate. How many beats will you count in each bar?	2
2	How many beats is each crotchet (♩) worth?	2
3	How many beats is the crotchet rest (𝄽) worth?	2
4	What is the letter name of the first note in bar 1? bar 2? bar 3?	2
5	What does *f (forte)* indicate?	2
6	What is the meaning of *Alla marcia*?	2
	Total:	12

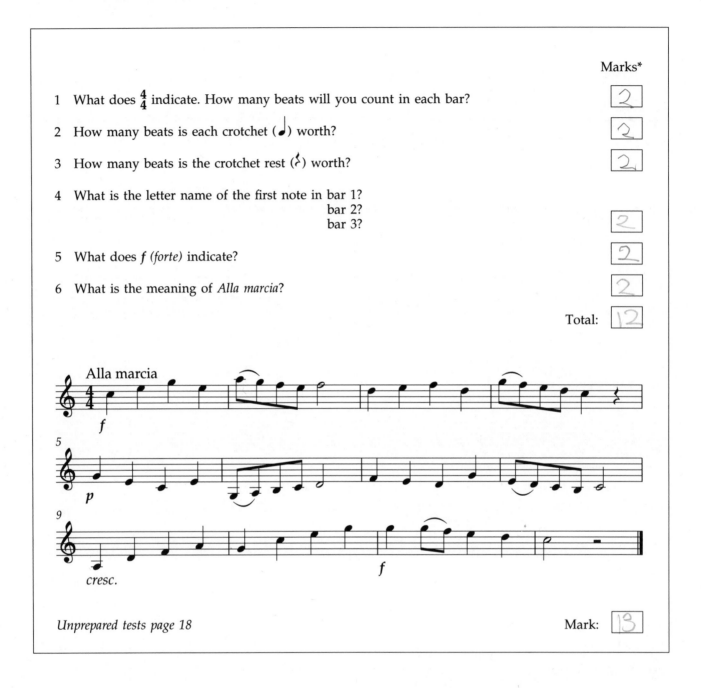

Unprepared tests page 18   Mark: 13

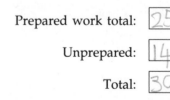

Prepared work total: 25

Unprepared: 14

Total: 39

*The mark boxes are to be filled in by your teacher (see Introduction).

24·03·05 (do scale of F)

STAGE 2

F major
More tied notes

RHYTHMIC EXERCISES

1

2

3

MELODIC EXERCISES

1

2

3

4

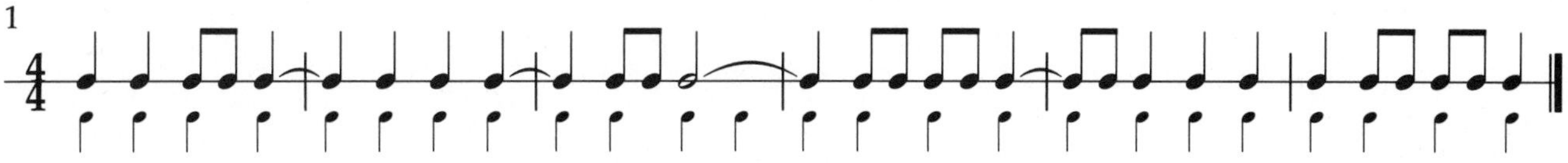

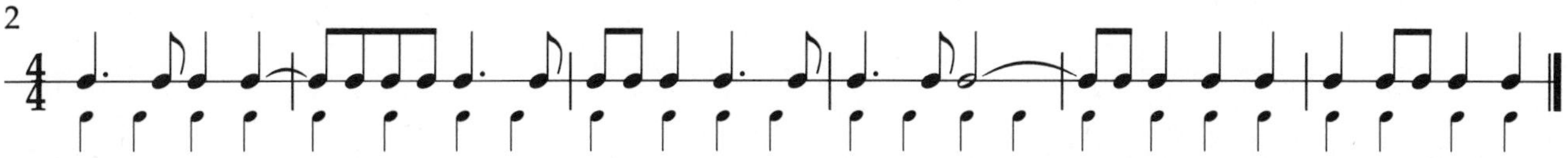

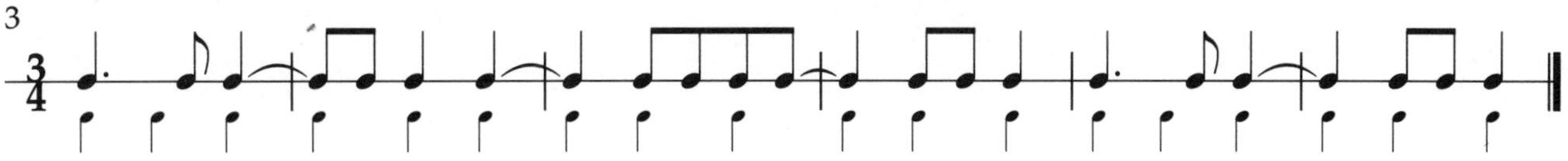

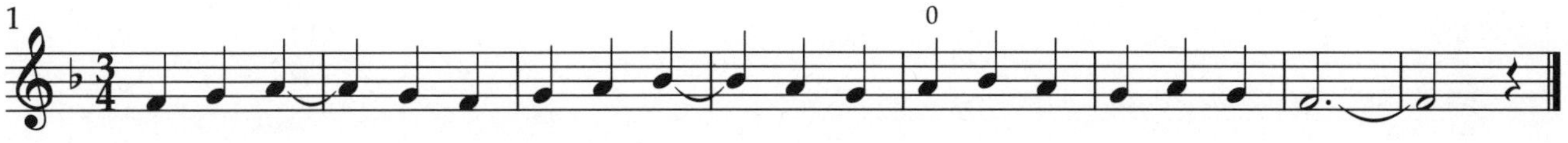

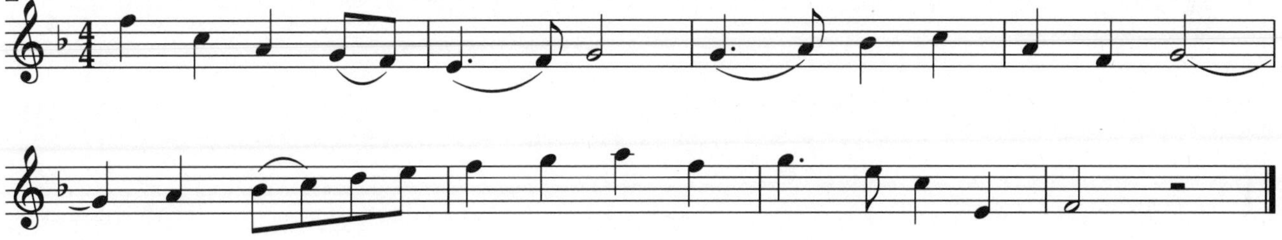

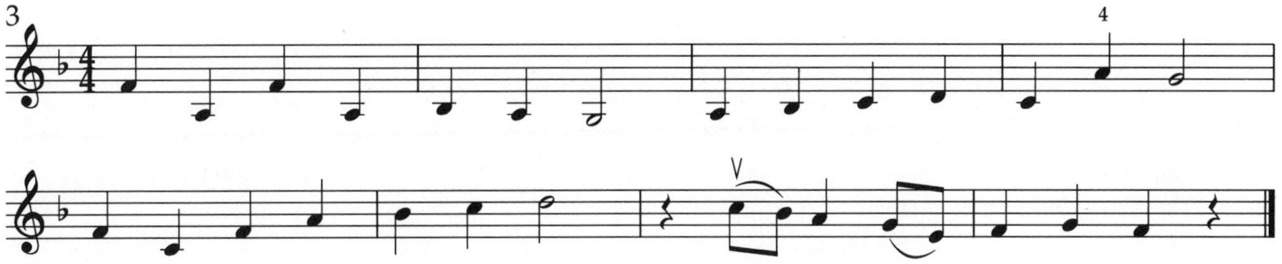

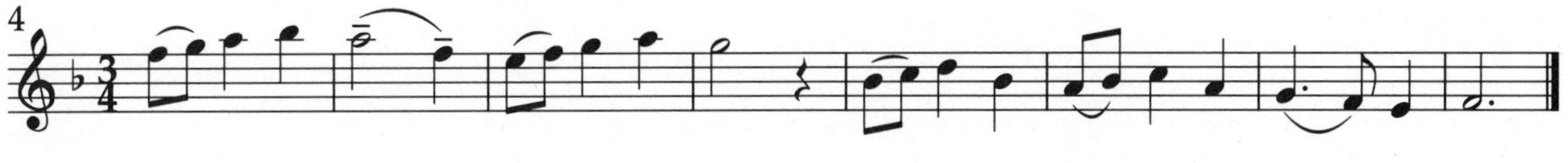

V.G.

PREPARED PIECE

1 What does *Con spirito* mean? `2`

2 Can you find two consecutive bars that have the same rhythm? `2`

3 What does the sign > in the last bar indicate? `2`

4 What does *rall.* mean? `2`

5 What will you count? `2`

6 In which key is this piece? `2`

Total: `2` 6

12

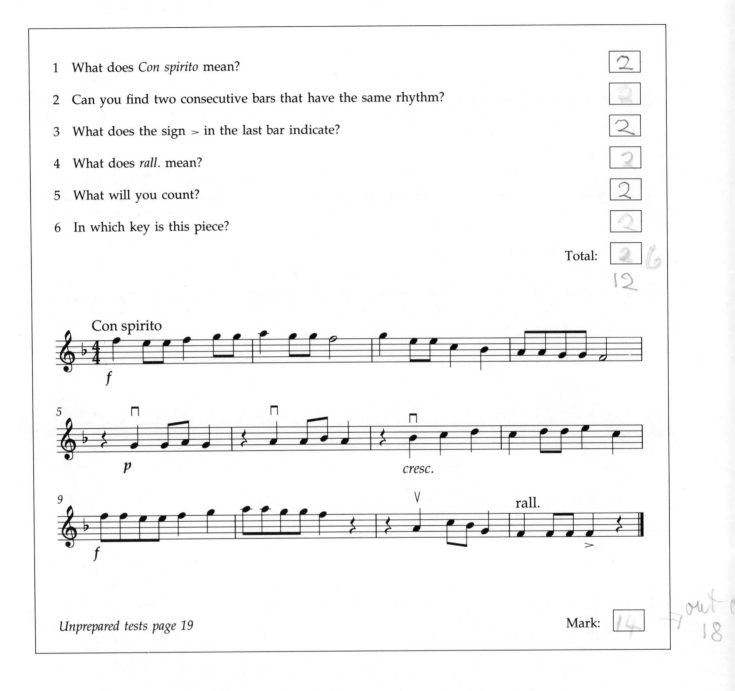

Unprepared tests page 19

Mark: `14` out of 18

Prepared work total: `26`

Unprepared: `15` out of 20

Total: `41`

Running totals:

1	2
39	41

28·04·05 Do one page, plus scale and arpeggio Also, revise F Major

STAGE 3

Bb Major

RHYTHMIC EXERCISES

MELODIC EXERCISES

PREPARED PIECE

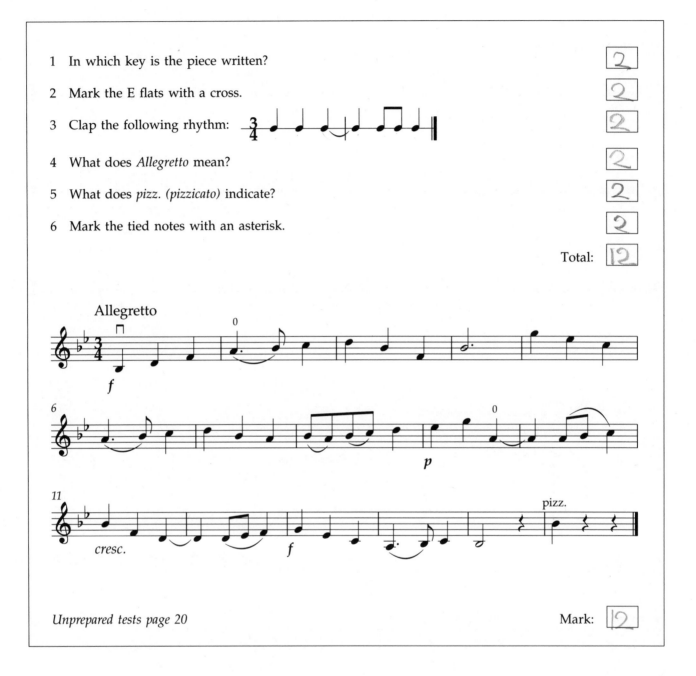

1 In which key is the piece written?   `2`

2 Mark the E flats with a cross.   `2`

3 Clap the following rhythm: `2`

4 What does *Allegretto* mean?   `2`

5 What does *pizz. (pizzicato)* indicate?   `2`

6 Mark the tied notes with an asterisk.   `2`

Total: `12`

Allegretto

Unprepared tests page 20

Mark: `12`

Prepared work total: `24`

Unprepared: `14`

Total: `38`

Running totals:

1	2	3
39	41	38

STAGE 4

A minor

RHYTHMIC EXERCISES

PREPARED PIECE

1 In which key is this piece written?

2 What does *Marziale* mean?

3 How will that marking affect your performance?

4 What does *dolce* mean and how will it affect your playing?

5 Where does the *Marziale* character return?

6 What does *poco a poco cresc.* mean?

Total:

Unprepared tests page 21

Mark:

Prepared work total:

Unprepared:

Total:

Running totals:

1	2	3	4

STAGE 5

D minor
4
8

RHYTHMIC EXERCISES

MELODIC EXERCISES

PREPARED PIECE

1 In which key is this piece written?

2 What is the character of this piece?

3 What does *p dolce* indicate?

4 Mark the first note affected by the key-signature.

5 How will you count this piece?

6 What does *rall.* mean?

Total:

Unprepared tests page 22

Mark:

Prepared work total:

Unprepared:

Total:

Running totals:

1	2	3	4	5

STAGE 6

RHYTHMIC EXERCISES

MELODIC EXERCISES

PREPARED PIECE

1   What does *Alla marcia* mean?

2   How will you give character to your performance?

3   What does the sign ᵒ indicate?

4   Clap the rhythm:

5   What will you count?

6   In which key is this piece?

Total:

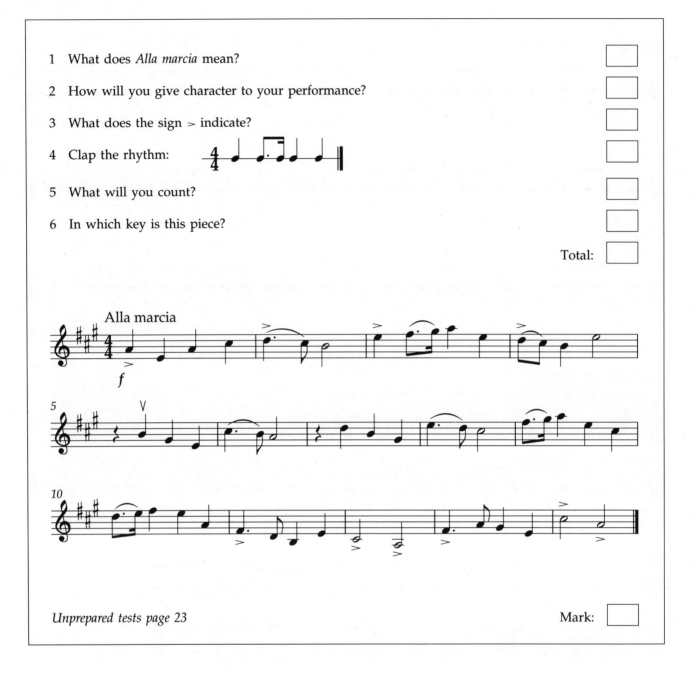

Alla marcia

Unprepared tests page 23

Mark:

Prepared work total:

Unprepared:

Total:

Running totals:

1	2	3	4	5	6

STAGE 7

G minor

RHYTHMIC EXERCISES

MELODIC EXERCISES

PREPARED PIECE

1 In which key is this piece written? `2`

2 What does *Molto espressivo* mean? `2`

3 How will that marking affect your performance? `2`

4 What does *dolce* mean? `2`

5 How will you count this piece? `2`

6 What does *poco a poco cresc.* mean? `2`

Total: `12`

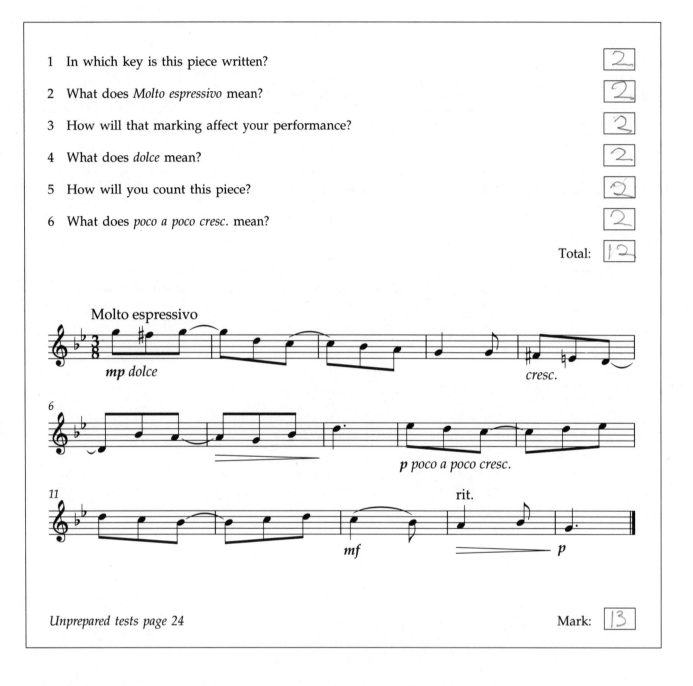

Unprepared tests page 24

Mark: `13`

Prepared work total: `25`

Unprepared: `94`

Total: `39`

Running totals:

1	2	3	4	5	6	7

CONCLUSION

A sight-reading checklist

Before you begin to play a piece at sight, always remember to consider the following:

1   Look at the key-signature.

2   Look at the time-signature, and decide how you will count the piece.

3   Notice any accidentals that may occur.

4   Notice any scale and arpeggio patterns.

5   Notice dynamic and other markings.

6   Look at the tempo mark and decide what speed to play.

7   Count one bar before you begin, to establish the speed.

When performing your sight-reading piece, always remember to:

1   CONTINUE TO COUNT THROUGHOUT THE PIECE.

2   Keep going at a steady and even tempo.

3   Ignore mistakes.

4   Check the key-signature at the beginning of each new line.

5   Look ahead – at least to the next beat or note.

6   Play *musically*.

UNPREPARED TESTS
STAGE 1

1 Hornpipe

2 Allegro moderato

3 Andantino

STAGE 2

1   Moderato

6

11   rall.

2   Allegretto grazioso

8

15

3   Andante

7

14   rit.

20

STAGE 3

1   Andante

mp   *cresc.*   *f*   *dim.*   *p*   *mf*

2   Allegro moderato

3   Allegro vigoroso

STAGE 4

1 Con spirito

2 Delicato

3 Marcato

STAGE 5

1   Con forza

9

2   Poco lento

9   rall.

3   Alla marcia

6

12

STAGE 6

1   Andante

2   Allegretto

3   Moderato con moto

STAGE 7

1   Adagio

2   Moderato

3   Allegro ma non troppo